THE MODERN FILIPINO

VOLUME TWO

NAVIGATING IDENTITY AS A FIRST-GENERATION IMMIGRANT

BAYANI CATAPANG

THE MODERN FILIPINO

Cover by Bayani Catapang

Illustrations by Bayani Catapang

Written by Bayani Catapang

DEDICATIONS

For my beloved family;

For my selected family – my friends;

For my Filipino kin, on home soil or abroad;

For the young pinoys and pinays;

For the allies of Filipinos; and

For the Filipino elders.

CONTENTS

PREFACE

The Modern Filipino is an autobiographical account of the life of a first-generation immigrant from the Philippines. The second volume of the series contains 15 chapters of oral storytelling, majority of which are based on personal experiences with the remainder based on shared histories between relatives. Each composition follows a 10-stanza format with differing word limit restrictions (with six, seven, or eight words per line). This volume covers a diverse range of topics, from the experiences of citizens who live in the provinces to the realities of the country's urban landscapes. There are several chapters in this volume that provide a critique on the current internal affairs of the Philippines with the intent of informing and inspiring meaningful dialogue. The experiences outlined in this book are not meant to be generalizations of the modern Filipino identity but rather a version of this persona transformed by the process of immigration.

1

FILIPINO SHAME

THEMES

Identity

Language

Dialect

Shame

Self-loathing

FORMAT

6 words per line

4 lines per stanza

10 stanzas total

RHYTHM

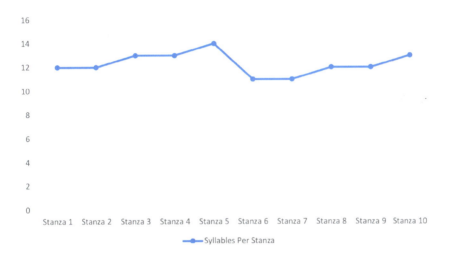

The following entry speaks to the linguistic diversity of the Philippines. Today, there are over 120 languages spoken in the archipelago. In Luzon, the northern island of the country, Bicolano, Ilocano, and Tagalog are the most common indigenous languages. In Visayas, the middle region of the archipelago (comprising various islands), Bisaya, Ilonggo, and Waray are the predominant indigenous languages of the region. In Mindanao, the southern landmass of the country, Bisaya, Cebuano, Ilonggo, and Tausug are the most commonly spoken indigenous languages. When the Spaniards colonized the islands in the 16th century, Spanish became the official language of the colony. When the United States of America claimed ownership of the Philippines, via the Treaty of Paris, English and Tagalog became the official languages. From a linguistic and historical standpoint, the proliferation of languages within the archipelago was highly influenced by local trade relations between different tribal groups and other nations.

[1]

The archipelago, blessed with many tongues

Priceless histories, erased and left unsung

Language variation, exclusive like each drum

Despite distinctiveness, what have we become?

[2]

A linguistic landscape, simplified into two:

Spanish or Tagalog, divide to misconstrue,

Marginalization with tact, a fruitless truth,

Our spirits' ego, disrespected without ruth.

[3]

With the original languages freely ignored,

Disregarded as dialects, a relentless reward,

Limited transparency with our freedom interred,

Ancestral wisdom they antagonize; left unheard.

[4]

Systematic silence transforming our nation's shame

Towards our heritage, depreciating our acclaim,

Our eventful history many cannot explain;

A timeless destruction, very little remains.

[5]

Eradicating our languages: a cultural death,

Accelerating to realization with every breath,

Demoralizing attacks, unrecognized for their depth,

Portraying the othered as intellectually inept.

[6]

The islanders' tongues diminished into one,

Segregation: can it ever be undone?

Ethnocentrism, regardless of how it's spun,

Forgotten relatives, those we brashly shun.

[7]

Retrograde, version two: the second chapter,

English or Tagalog, our second master,

Adapting to appease our newest captors,

To ensure survival despite dire factors.

[8]

With the other languages devalued, demeaned,

Knowledge concealed: but has anyone intervened?

Our citizens who navigate the in-between,

English prominence in the government machine.

[9]

Children unaware of our country's innocence,

Hindering our efforts to maintain diligence,

An era of rampant cognitive dissonance,

Ignorant to the struggle: lacking vigilance.

[10]

The generations attempting to engage rapport

Communicates with anger, challenging the score,

How much peripheralization must we endure?

Investigate ourselves by resisting the allure.

2

FILIPINO VACATION

THEMES

Expectations

Extravagance

Impudence

Guilt

Compassion

FORMAT

7 words per line

4 lines per stanza

10 stanzas total

RHYTHM

The following entry speaks to the experience of a Filipino immigrant who visits family after being away for many years. The level of poverty in this developing nation is far removed from the definition of poverty seen in first world countries. Typically, Filipinos who overcame poverty and were able to immigrate to a more prosperous nation become the breadwinners of the entire family tree. In 2019, it was estimated that over 12 million Filipinos live abroad. Today, it remains commonplace for immigrants to send money to their families on a monthly basis. Philippine government studies have estimated that at least 10% of the country's Gross Domestic Product comes from money sent by relatives living overseas. In 2022, one Canadian dollar is equivalent to approximately 43 Philippine pesos, so money sent to the Philippines goes a very long way and can transform the lives of those who still live there today.

[1]

Luna visits relatives after many years away,

An expensive vacation under the family's sway,

To victimize the visitor, sanity they betray,

Masquerading manners with the insolence they portray.

[2]

A shameless arrogance seen at the restaurant,

With extravagant orders; the numbers surely daunt,

She manufactures debt, supplying all their wants,

Unable to refuse, she tolerates their taunts.

[3]

Now at the mall after demonstrating gluttony,

The relatives carry on in disgraced company,

Filling their carts and using restraint reluctantly,

Paying it forward, controlling her tongue, sullenly.

[4]

After arriving home from a full excursion,

The other relatives report with their coercion,

Rows of family members past the horizons,

Begging for money before their status worsens.

[5]

Unable to refuse those often set apart,

Kindness and compassion filled Luna's bleeding heart,

By forcing her to overcommit and contort,

The heartstrings they manipulate and now extort.

[6]

A monumental undertaking to frequent the home,

Revisiting our previous lives; enjoying the roam,

Family members forgotten, many of them unknown,

Distant relatives that bow to imaginary thrones.

[7]

At the restaurant overpowered by true instinct,

Eating quality food on a memorable stint,

With full transparency, no requirement to squint;

Dishonoured by indigence, she understood the hint.

[8]

Exploring the mall after satiating their hunger,

The schoolkids gather with their stationery rosters,

Parents with their progeny behaving like monsters,

Weaponizing their children with a brazen valour.

[9]

At the family household the traveler rests

In between summons from the uninvited guests,

Most asking for cash, empathy they overstress,

Withholding support would leave many in distress.

[10]

Complete understanding of the hardship at hand,

Once intimate with poverty in the homeland,

An unintended consequence none of us planned,

To abandon our families, should we be damned?

3

FILIPINO SELECTION

THEMES

Family

Scarcity

Jealousy

Obligation

Sacrifice

FORMAT

8 words per line

4 lines per stanza

10 stanzas total

RHYTHM

The following entry speaks to the experience of a poor Filipino family living in the provinces. Although the Philippines is considered a developing nation, many regions have not caught up with modernization. Today, city life remains a sharp contrast to provincial life. Many families in the provinces provide for themselves by living off the land, fishing on local bodies of water, or planting fruits and vegetables on their family plots. Although public education is funded by the government, school equipment like uniforms and stationery are expensive commodities that many citizens cannot afford: in fact, it is common for poor families to remove their children from public school once they are able to join the workforce as labourers. Moreover, it is typical for families of the lower class with multiple children to select only one child to obtain further education (past secondary school) as a direct result of their financial circumstances.

[1]

A young couple discusses the future in tears,

Labouring for their children and their dream careers,

Surviving the hardship: a life that is severe,

The elites prosper while they drain the austere.

[2]

After deep contemplation they tasked the female child

To rescue everyone from poverty, from the wild,

Chosen to study in school, the rest unreconciled,

Living devoid of knowledge: the human soul defiled.

[3]

The three brothers agonize abandoned in the background,

Aware of their misfortune, a resentment they compound

With jealousy and anger and bitterness all around

From sibling rivalry, a repeat story, one renowned.

[4]

By completing her program, a true life achievement,

The buzzer starts ticking to reverse the mistreatment,

Now obliged to provide for their many requirements,

She settles all the bills; showing no disagreement.

[5]

A truly heavy burden she's required to pay

To transform her family's lives day after day,

Her personal wants and needs, she often betrays,

Relentless endurance, as long as she can pray.

[6]

With little cash the household of six endures,

Betting it all on one ticket, clearly obscure,

They weighed their options, limited chances for sure,

Having no agency for them to feel secure.

[7]

The daughter is determined: ignoring all the pain,

Conquering all the obstacles by using her brain,

She sacrifices her sleep in order to obtain

A higher quality of life within their domain.

[8]

The roster of concessions from the brothers forgotten,

Vilifying their sister because of their envy: rotten,

Abused as their wallet, an experience so common,

With a sister they unabashedly treat as foreign.

[9]

After years of excellence to finish her degree,

Now the family collects: how could she disagree?

By taking her freedom they're unable to see

The family trauma: a present for the unfree.

[10]

In spite of fatigue, she continues to persist,

Reject the abundance, so they can all subsist,

With zero choice, she denies herself and resists

A life of luxury, to survive and coexist.

4

FILIPINO FREEDOM

THEMES

Transference

Neglect

Resentment

Hatred

Indifference

FORMAT

6 words per line

4 lines per stanza

10 stanzas total

<u>RHYTHM</u>

The following entry speaks to the experience of a Filipino child who is neglected by his father. In the modern Filipino first-generation immigrant story, what typically happens is one parent immigrates overseas on a working visa while the other stays home and assumes the role of both parents until the entire family reunites abroad. Although not a cardinal rule, it is more common for the mothers to immigrate for work, leaving behind the fathers - who typically are not skilled at conservative matriarchal responsibilities - to provide both emotional and financial support to the children. When fathers disregard these important obligations, the task of caring for the children is often delegated to a close relative, like their own parents (i.e., the children's grandparents). In the best case scenario, relatives step in and fill in the gaps of a fragmented family, and in the worst, a childhood is wasted due to parental neglect.

[1]

The firstborn child, a spitting image,

A carbon copy of his visage,

Rejected child left in the village,

Kinship kindness he has to pillage.

[2]

His basic needs the father fulfils,

The bare minimum: paying the bills,

A short temper and limited chill,

Respecting his rules, his every will.

[3]

Raising his child with little affection,

Upholding the customs of our nation,

Thriving despite a life of frustration,

Masking his pain with bogus emotion.

[4]

Watch how resentment turns into hatred,

Directed at the son he created,

A life of freedom, considered sacred,

Ceased to exist, now completely jaded.

[5]

A paternal love mixed with indifference,

Stubbornness due to a childlike innocence,

Drowning himself in his own magnificence,

He navigates life with true ignorance.

[6]

The son follows suit, directly behind,

Searching for acceptance, a fruitless find,

Precarious living: a state of mind,

A life of insanity, one unkind.

[7]

Callous love, a repeat of history?

Was his upbringing filled with misery?

Did he suffer in the periphery?

A life story shrouded in mystery.

[8]

With obligations that serve to inhibit

His primal impulses, all too explicit,

Achieving his goals with parental limits,

Resenting his child - restraining his spirit.

[9]

With a childhood separated from the rest,

The son is disregarded; zero protest,

Lacking agency, not able to contest

His father's mistreatment: a nonage arrest.

[10]

With pride, prejudice, and blatant audacity,

The father continues with his voracity,

Justifying his deeds removed from morality,

Prioritizing his dreams: the youth's mentality.

5

FILIPINO DIVORCE

THEMES

Mediation

Betrayal

Hatred

Revenge

Consequences

FORMAT

7 words per line

4 lines per stanza

10 stanzas total

RHYTHM

The following entry speaks to the experience of a Filipino child who has to serve as a mediator for his embittered parents. Even today, infidelity remains a classic cause of divorce; when combined with the separation and uncertainty that comes with a long-distance marriage, it can lead to the breakdown of a fragmented family unit. When children are placed in the crossfire of disputes between parents, their childhoods often become collateral damage. Although kids virtually lack all forms of agency, they are sometimes used by their parents as a means of communication, acting as a messenger pigeon from one to the other. During this process, children are prematurely exposed to the realities of life and the complexities of interpersonal relations. While some children are enabled to enjoy the niceties of a healthy family life, those from broken households have to fill in the many voids created by a broken family.

[1]

The firstborn child is the true mediator

For his parent's divorce, their peace translator,

Dealing with both sides, the child arbitrator

Looks into the faults of the fornicator.

[2]

The faithful mother that he often betrayed

Fell out of love: indifference he portrayed,

A real philanderer, even if she prayed,

Indulging his penis, every week he strayed.

[3]

An all-consuming love in its truest form

Turned into loathing: trapped inside a storm

Of kinship treason - such a common norm

In our home country, one that needs reform.

[4]

After years of sorrow, she wants revenge

On her partner: abhorrence she must quench,

Repulsion on sight, she planned to avenge

Her pure virtue against the wretched wench.

[5]

The son, lost in the family feud,

Numbs his conscience while masking his mood,

A childhood theft, learning to be shrewd,

While facing all the pain that ensued.

[6]

A deep understanding of his father's sin,

Investigating the facts: none of them wins,

From ripe adolescence he toughens his skin,

Predicting hardship - now a new life begins.

[7]

In the turmoil they discussed his infractions

And the reasons for his repulsive actions,

Begging his wife with the following question:

"What if polygamy could be an option?"

[8]

Stuck in the world of the subjective,

But without guilt, could he be reflective?

With his logic he states his perspective,

And pleads for her to remain objective.

[9]

She rejected the offer, he fought back

By leaving his kids: a callous attack,

With zero chance he would ever backtrack,

He gifts his family much to unpack.

[10]

Choosing to heal, they trust each other,

And brave the storm; mending their honour,

In their new lives without a father,

The son steps up - a loving brother.

6

FILIPINO ABUSE

THEMES

Disagreement

Conflict

Anger

Assault

Arrest

FORMAT

8 words per line

4 lines per stanza

10 stanzas total

RHYTHM

The following entry speaks to the experience of a Filipino wife who is finally able to stand up to the mistreatment of her husband. In patriarchal societies such as the Philippines, women can become victims in their marriage if their husbands exert toxic control over their household. In the Philippines, it remains a tradition for the man to lead the household, which can minimize the agency of women to influence their own lives. To a strict traditionalist, immigrating to a different country can become emasculating when their values are challenged in a new environment that places more emphasis on gender equality. Aside from the Vatican, the Philippines remains the only country that outlaws absolute divorce, a restriction that contributes to the continued emotional, financial, or physical abuse experienced by the wives of abusive husbands. Even today, marital abuse is one of the reasons some women leave their husbands after immigrating.

[1]

After a year goes by, the quarrels begin,

The father and mother, their patience wear thin;

With a mother's courage and very thick skin,

She awakens his wrath, causing him to sin.

[2]

In this country, women are given equal rights,

The welcome advantage of taking the big flight,

A power inequity that she brings to light:

Now the wife is finally empowered to fight.

[3]

Unable to adapt to his new life's dynamic

Provokes a toxic temper with a true panic,

After losing his composure, he acts all manic,

Before raising his fist in full anger: volcanic.

[4]

To mix surprise with his fury and virulence,

He pushes her down, consumed by his truculence,

She fights for survival; he disrupts the silence

Clobbering his wife in a burst of violence.

[5]

Throughout their marriage he's never been this rough,

But with this act, she's finally had enough,

Struggling for her life she pushes him off

And scurries up the stairs; she's certainly tough.

[6]

In the Philippines, she turned the other cheek,

Here in Canada, she is no longer meek,

After years of restraint, now able to speak,

To express her feelings: she was never weak.

[7]

In previous fights, she was cornered, all alone,

Surrounded by vultures that live to throw stones;

But in this paradise, everything is made known

With impartial justice, and now he must atone.

[8]

Given a short-term sentence for his passionate crime,

To re-examine his actions while doing his time,

Was he missing his independence and youthful prime?

Did he scrutinize his character in this downtime?

[9]

After the handcuffs, the police questioned the son

Who witnessed the assault, everything he had done;

Traumatized in complete shock with nowhere to run

From rampant abuse that can never be undone.

[10]

Despising the deed that led to the arrest,

The son adds to memories, those he detests;

Blessed with a husband, the source of unrest,

She asked for a divorce - a cogent request.

7

FILIPINO EMERGENCY

THEMES

Immigration

Assimilation

Obligation

Helplessness

Security

FORMAT

6 words per line

4 lines per stanza

10 stanzas total

RHYTHM

The following entry speaks to the experience of a Filipino immigrant family who has to balance religious obligations and daily expenses while also financially supporting family members in the Philippines. Many Filipino immigrants congregate at religious institutions as a means of building a social network in a new country. In these churches, newly-arrived immigrants bond over religion as well as the condition of being a first-generation immigrant. In fact, it is not uncommon for immigrants to seek out religious communities - even from their home countries prior to moving - as a means to preserve their ability to speak their mother tongues and safeguard their cultural practices. Today, many Filipinos abroad are able to keep in contact with their family members back home because of the spread of technology and modern infrastructure. It is unfortunate that many Filipino immigrants only receive phone calls from their family members because they need financial help.

[1]

Unified through faith, a young family

Leaves the homeland in tears happily,

Five lonely years they endured silently,

Speaking to God, they prayed religiously.

[2]

They join an Asian church community

Keen to bond with other minorities,

Self-love and kindness, their new realities,

Framing the self with new identities.

[3]

Despite comforts their life is austere,

Balancing the bills, tithing in fear,

Afraid for family they hold dear

Who live through poverty every year.

[4]

Everyday struggles to pay the rent,

Limited options, no time to vent,

Resisting all wants for every cent,

With one payment everything is spent.

[5]

Special requests not made with ease,

With a quick phone call overseas,

Dialing the number is their key,

To gain favours on bended knees.

[6]

A relative pleads for our compassion,

Suppressing sobs in a frantic fashion,

Having no money to act, inaction,

Begging for cash with no satisfaction.

[7]

A tragic event, one hot afternoon,

Ploughing ricefields as the children prune,

Serpents bite when timing is opportune;

In the mountains, nobody is immune.

[8]

A preteen is hit, venomous strike,

Clinging to life, the fever spikes,

They leave the village; treacherous hike,

Dreading the prices with much dislike.

[9]

At the hospital making the call,

Without any choice the parents bawl,

Feeling so powerless, up the wall,

Sorrow with anger, ready to brawl.

[10]

Phone calls that bring terrible news,

Life or death, the immigrants choose,

Without option, they pay the dues,

A tax from blood: kinship abuse.

8

FILIPINO SPIDER

THEMES

Childhood

Nature

Hunting

Competition

Gambling

FORMAT

7 words per line

4 lines per stanza

10 stanzas total

RHYTHM

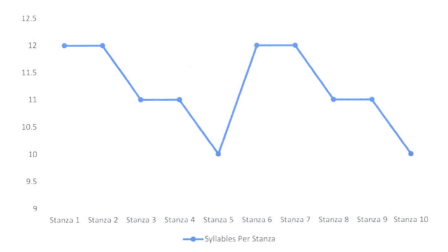

The following entry speaks to the experience of Filipino children playing with their spider toys. The cultural event of hosting a spider derby is more commonly seen in provincial regions, away from the cosmopolitan zones of the country. Even today, a childhood spent in the provinces remains a stark contrast to one spent in the modern urban landscapes of the Philippines. While city kids enjoy and perpetuate modern sports like basketball or soccer, children in the provinces safeguard traditional Filipino games like Sunka (a board game) or Luksong Tinik (a jumping competition), amongst many others. In the cities, children have to learn about specific neighbourhoods and city landmarks; however, in the provinces children have to embrace nature and everything that comes with it. The incorporation of betting to spider derbies is a recent phenomenon in Filipino history: this cultural shift took place in the early 2000s amongst other social improvements.

[1]

The Filipino children are gathered, they cheer

Immersed in the customs of provincial pioneers,

Educated from five to explore without fear,

Searching for spiders in the superlative tier.

[2]

In the vast forest, within the vegetation

The strong spiders thrive, they surpass expectations;

Young kids hunting, armed with ancient information,

Chasing after fame to build a reputation.

[3]

Watch as you harvest the venomous spider,

They do defend themselves from all outsiders,

Look for the webs: the nourishment provider,

Strength and sheen are the initial deciders.

[4]

Inside the ring, the ferocious spiders shine,

A soldier on separate sides by design,

Fighting for survival while threading the line,

The referee decides and gives the sign.

[5]

Children are waiting to collect their bets,

There are winners - but many are upset;

If they succeed they will never forget,

Some find happiness while others find debt.

[6]

Visiting the provinces, going back in time,

Forgetting our origins is a modern crime,

Children are disciplined to tolerate the grime,

Living in modesty, despite the daily climb.

[7]

Grateful for the mountains and magnificent shores,

Timeless elegance that no one should ignore,

Reconnoitering the wild is never a bore,

Adapting to the environment more and more.

[8]

The children scatter, inspecting all the trees

And common greenery, they traverse with ease,

Procuring warriors that fetch quite a fee,

But before combat, starvation is the key.

[9]

Handlers servicing their spiders in a box,

Before the duel the many viewers flock,

The fight commences: some applaud, others mock,

Introduction to the battle of the cocks.

[10]

Children betting, they share the local joys,

Raised with nature away from city noise,

Social cohesion: all the girls and boys

Have great contentment in their spider toys.

9

FILIPINO STAPLE

THEMES

Air

Fire

Water

Earth

Spirit

FORMAT

8 words per line

4 lines per stanza

10 stanzas total

RHYTHM

The following entry speaks to the experience of Filipino rice farmers who live in the provinces of the country. In terms of economic and social importance, the planting and harvesting of rice remains an essential activity for the Philippines. Like in most Asian countries, rice is a staple resource for Filipino citizens. Even today, agricultural zones where rice is grown (amongst other staples like banana, corn, and pineapple) remain concentrated in the peripheral provincial regions away from the cosmopolitan zones of the country, where real estate is sparse. With the continued proliferation of poverty in the country, the issue of food insecurity grows more significant with the ever-increasing population boom of the archipelago. Government studies conducted in 2021 have estimated that approximately 18% of Filipino citizens currently live below the poverty threshold; in a population of an estimated 111 million, this amounts to approximately 20 million citizens regularly experiencing starvation.

[1]

The daily sunrise makes the family roosters crow,

Waking the household, keeping everyone on their toes,

Our mountain provinces, bathed in a glistening glow

Gifts the inhabitants the essential crops it grows.

[2]

The shimmering sepia tone of the smouldering sun

Invites the peaceful spirits to enjoy the fun;

Before planting seedlings we savour a morning bun,

Remembering our tales, how our story had begun.

[3]

The rivers and waterfalls that nurture us all

Feed the families of the modern mountain sprawl,

Although we lack altitude, blessed to be small,

We live in humility and answer the call.

[4]

The nutritious soil that sustains our holy rice

Is a priceless treasure, the old sage advice,

With discipline and diligence, we pay the price,

Deserving of the harvest, grateful to the skies.

[5]

The souls of our ancestors watching us thrive,

Living in nature like when they were alive,

If you listen gently, let your faith revive;

Whispers will echo - just let your instincts drive.

[6]

The insects are synchronized, everyone is in tune,

Small crickets welcoming the arrival of the moon,

Even on the rainy months, our seasonal monsoons,

Mating summons fill the air from early afternoon.

[7]

The faithful forest dwellers, enveloped by the hue

Of generous Saint Luna from a heavenly view,

Blessings from the universe, so eternal and true,

Shower the village citizens, bonding them like glue.

[8]

The evenings attract the rainfall from far away,

It quenches the thirsty woodlands, day after day,

Watering the topsoil where all the creatures play,

Feeding the denizens who still live there today.

[9]

Green paddies change colour into a golden brown,

They gather the people throughout the happy town,

Celebrating the reaping; no one with a frown,

Our sacred mother Gaia, her bounty is renown.

[10]

The beings that protect us from far beyond,

Send us best wishes but we cannot respond,

Death is not an issue for eternal bonds;

Even in the afterlife, our kin are fond.

10

FILIPINO SPORT

THEMES

Dedication

Cohesion

Competition

Victory

Defeat

FORMAT

6 words per line

4 lines per stanza

10 stanzas total

RHYTHM

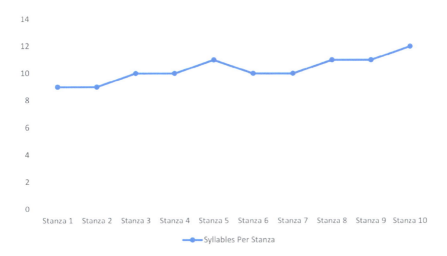

The following entry speaks to the cultural phenomenon of Cockfighting (colloquially known as the "Sabong"), popular in the provincial regions of the Philippines. Although it is illegal in many countries, this pastime remains largely unregulated in this nation. As a cultural practice, it existed in the archipelago before the arrival of the Spaniards: there are historical records from 1521 sourced from Ferdinand Magellan's chroniclers that document the ancient sport. Even in the early 2000s, cockfighting derbies were a popular gambling activity for many adults (mostly men - however, these days there are more women becoming involved in the activity). As a result of the country's recent modernization, online gambling on cockfighting derbies has become a significant economic activity: in 2022, it brought an estimated 650 million Philippine pesos every month from government-facilitated online betting platforms. This figure does not include the funds raised from unregulated cockfighting derbies in the provincial regions.

[1]

Roosters crowing before the morning fight,

Claiming the terrain - their natural right;

From the beginning, they proudly invite

Other chickens to scuffle with might.

[2]

At the venue, the masses congregate,

Financial statuses left at the gate,

Before entering, forget all the hate:

In this battle, everyone must relate.

[3]

Owner with soldier, a fine combination,

Connected through will for the situation,

Before the match, with ample preparation,

Spurs are enhanced with little hesitation.

[4]

After you dominate, the spectators cheer

Celebrating your victory - loud and clear,

Your reputation within the local sphere

Is cemented in the underground frontier.

[5]

After losing, your family members embrace,

Destroying your self-esteem; the people debase,

Without surrendering, determined to save face,

The overpowered are rewarded with disgrace.

[6]

In the morning the fighter prepares:

Awake before daybreak, saying his prayers,

The family investment made with care,

When triumphant, he flourishes with flair.

[7]

At the locale, the warriors cavort,

Sharpening their blades: their life support,

Inside the cage, the referee reports

The victors of this Filipino sport.

[8]

Money is collected before every game,

Players pay admission, regardless of fame,

Outside the arena, the owners exclaim,

Shouting battle cries for provincial acclaim.

[9]

After a victory, the arbiter speaks,

Offering his wisdom and his critiques,

Entrants take notes on every technique,

Debated in the battleground, every week.

[10]

The champion collects, the defeated retreats,

One with accolades: the cockfighting elite,

Failures awarded nothing except the meat:

A bittersweet aftertaste upon a defeat.

11

FILIPINO WATERFALL

<u>THEMES</u>

Preparation

Travel

Water

Wildlife

Solidarity

<u>FORMAT</u>

7 words per line

4 lines per stanza

10 stanzas total

RHYTHM

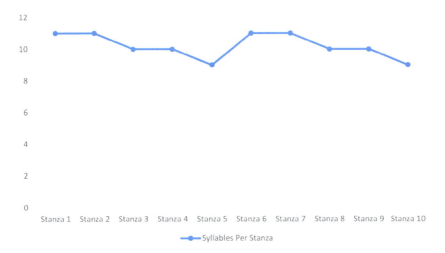

The following entry speaks to the experience of a Filipino family that pays a visit to a sacred waterfall hidden from most outsiders. Although there are over 3,100 known cave formations in the Philippines, there remain many sites that have yet to be surveyed and officially catalogued by the government. Even today, many indigenous communities safeguard the locations of various natural features to prevent further government development projects that would exploit these treasures for monetary gain. In Luzon alone, the northern landmass of the archipelago, there are over 450 known cave formations documented by the government. When precious resources like gold and silver are found in these locations, government entities and criminal organizations often claim ownership over these territories. During these power struggles, the inhabitants of these regions are often caught in the crossfire and displaced. Unfortunately, when it comes to firepower, criminal groups are often superior to the government.

[1]

The children are excited: the evening before,

Preparing for an adventure, rarely a bore,

Inside the mountains that we frequently explore

We endeavour to replenish our inner cores.

[2]

A dangerous expedition to find the site,

The family waterfall is our secret right,

Within the mountainsides, we follow the light,

Revealing our holy caves - such a delight.

[3]

A pristine waterfall isolated from the rest,

We safeguard the mountains, our spiritual test,

The groundwater is crystal clear, everyone attests,

Unparalleled elegance - what else can you request?

[4]

The curious fish are undisturbed, graciously free,

Living their lives peacefully in natural glee,

Exclusive to the mountaineers, the elder's decree,

A sacred sanctuary - a rarity to see.

[5]

To complete the preparations, our annual retreat:

Participants must contribute before taking a seat,

Regulated by nature we relinquish all conceit,

Appreciate the universe - the number one elite.

[6]

Before returning home, we scrutinize the scene,

Revering the mountain is our daily routine,

Concerted efforts to keep the area clean,

Protecting our haven, away from the obscene.

[7]

We traverse the formation, marching without fear,

Our elders navigate while the ancestors steer,

Ignoring the cold water, we all persevere,

A timeless pilgrimage we observe every year.

[8]

The shimmering mountain water purifies with ease,

Filling the faithful citizens with unrivalled peace,

A respected resource that everyone must police,

Superlative importance, or else we risk disease.

[9]

Due to our avarice and human confrontations,

The balance is skewed, without any conversations,

Subjected to the will of human devastation,

Our wildlife is threatened by selfish corporations.

[10]

To conserve the wilderness, the inhabitants refuse

And resist all "development", a "justified" abuse,

Caretakers of our history, recognizing the ruse,

Ensuring our survival - we investigate their views.

12

FILIPINO INGENUITY

<u>THEMES</u>

Survival

Resourcefulness

Persistence

Humility

Awareness

<u>FORMAT</u>

8 words per line

4 lines per stanza

10 stanzas total

RHYTHM

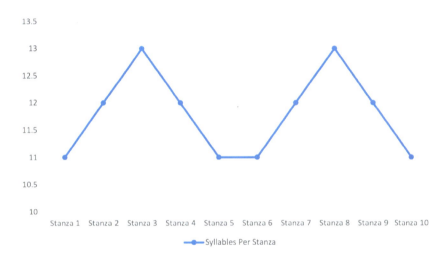

The following entry speaks to the experience of Filipino children who live in or near cemetery plots. For many homeless families, cemeteries have become a common living environment out of necessity. In the densely populated regions of the Philippines like Manila, cemetery slums have existed since the 1950s. Although less common, this phenomenon is also seen in the provincial regions of the country. When homeless citizens illegally convert private burial plots into their homes, law enforcement organizations like the municipal police face significant issues when enforcing the law because of the overcrowding of local penitentiaries and the severe backlog of criminal court cases awaiting trial. Where opportunities or resources are scarce, the impoverished must adapt to their environment, and this often means creating unconventional sources of income. Due to the cycle of disadvantage, surviving in dire conditions becomes a family affair where children are incorporated into the family's economic endeavours.

[1]

Morning or evening, you see them all flock

To find all the goodies, the local stock:

A herd of children run around the block,

Having their fun but always on the clock.

[2]

The children pair up and assess the scene,

Despite hardship they think the grass is green,

Candles for meals: a day-to-day routine,

If it is a crime, who will intervene?

[3]

The children then gather to combine their wax,

When the pot is full everyone can relax;

A fire is ignited while watching their backs,

Melting the candles to make money for snacks.

[4]

Children are waiting for their candles to dry,

Mixed with darker pigments so people would buy,

When the relatives come to visit and cry,

They light many candles and feed the supply.

[5]

On the regular, they pray to God, confessing,

Asking for mercy, in case they were transgressing;

In the afternoon the children count their earnings,

Working in the system while hiding their yearning.

[6]

Our festival of The Day of The Dead,

When the kin visit, the spirits break bread,

The kids are thrilled - consumed by healthy dread,

Slaving away to climb out of the red.

[7]

The adults cook and the giddy kids sell

While mingling with the crowd - ringing their bells,

"Balut! Balut!" is what they have to yell

For peddling this treat, heaven in a shell.

[8]

Grinding for cash to add to the salary,

With an extra long shift, many are merry,

Filling their backpacks with all they can carry,

The kids walk the beat of the cemetery.

[9]

From the early evening and up until late,

The kids share the burden: distribute the weight,

Before midnight hits they meet around the gate,

Celebrating their night with food on the plate.

[10]

Early in the morning they combine the proceeds

From their eventful evening, did the kids succeed?

The dedicated effort they give for their needs

Is actioned for the collective - with love, indeed.

13

FILIPINO GAMBLER

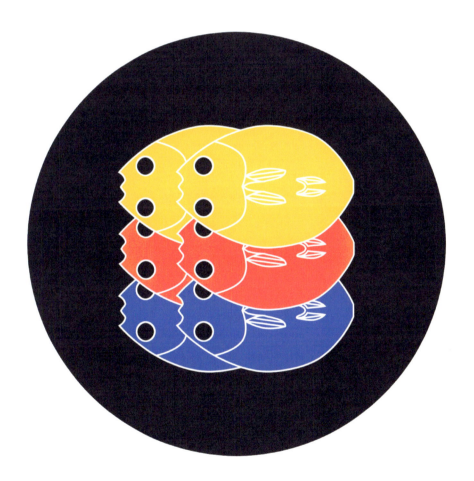

<u>THEMES</u>

Gambling

Frustration

Abuse

Freedom

Celebration

<u>FORMAT</u>

6 words per line

4 lines per stanza

10 stanzas total

RHYTHM

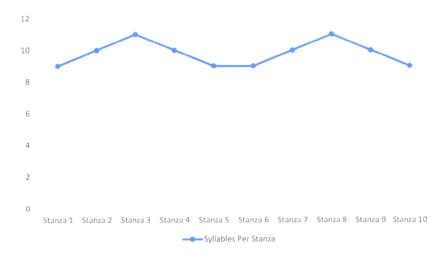

The following entry speaks to the practice of drinking and gambling amongst adults, a popular pastime for Filipino society. In the Philippines, gambling can take many forms; however, traditional card games like Pusoy Dos (Filipino Big Two) or Tong Its remain popular choices. Regardless of economic stature, a game of cards is often accompanied by monetary risk, as Filipinos love to gamble. In these competitions, people may lose their expendable income - which can have a drastic impact on participants with family obligations. Although some players could win big during these local competitions, many individuals go into debt because of their addiction to gambling. When large bets are lost, participants can resort to outrage and violence. From a young age, Filipino children become proficient in traditional card games, and upon entry to the income-producing workforce, many mirror the actions of relatives and make the easy transition to gambling and alcohol consumption.

[1]

Village drunkards playing with their cards,

A social norm: fighting for rewards,

No regards, relaxing in the yard,

Smoking and drinking, quitting is hard.

[2]

In the mania of Filipino streets,

Mathematicians are the ones to beat

After a night of financial defeat,

The losers walk home, feeling incomplete.

[3]

Lacking willpower to cancel or abort,

Jeopardizing their pay: a national sport,

Grown men bonding, the original cohort

Encouraging each other while they cavort.

[4]

Habits nurtured by their older brothers,

Following the steps of their forefathers,

Restraining all logic to find honour,

Without question, they accept the collar.

[5]

After winning, they revel in fame,

With good company fanning the flame,

The youth's conceit, maddening to tame,

Feeding narcissism, all for the game.

[6]

Breadwinners gather to grab a bite,

Drinking beer with smokes every night,

At the start, everyone is polite,

Speak incorrectly: it's time to fight.

[7]

Losers bickering as the poison spreads,

Resulting from egos that are overfed,

Aggression from the table to the bed,

Collateral damage: stuck in the red.

[8]

Family casualties: wives battered and bruised,

With kids witnessing, terrified and confused,

Rewriting history, their truths are subdued,

Terror of the collective left unpursued.

[9]

Anger that waters the family tree

Leads to resentment, it's a guarantee;

Meekness programmed, it's difficult to flee

Belligerent fathers: should we break free?

[10]

With no one willing to intercede,

Silence is best, until they secede,

After a loss the family bleeds,

But when he wins, everyone succeeds.

14

FILIPINO GOSSIP

THEMES

Silence

Secrecy

Shame

Abuse

Hypocrisy

FORMAT

7 words per line

4 lines per stanza

10 stanzas total

RHYTHM

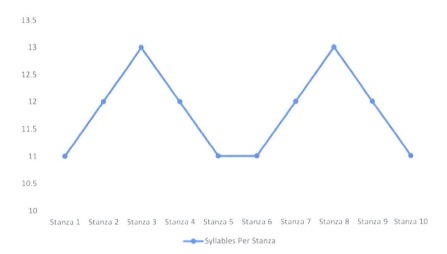

The following entry speaks to the experience of a Filipino family surviving the abuse of their patriarch. For many traditional families of the Philippines, involvement in a Christian church community is a social imperative. Sometimes churches are the only spaces that new immigrants can access in a foreign country. When family relations are healthy, the church community can serve to improve an immigrant family's quality of life; conversely, when there is turmoil in the family unit, there is a chance that an overbearing religious community can further degrade the well-being of suffering families. Since Christians place great importance on the survival of the nuclear family, sometimes these religious communities enable the cycle of abuse experienced by spouses or children because they advocate for reconciliation instead of divorce. With the message of Christianity being that all confessed sins are forgiven by God, many abusive fathers experience leniency outside of mandated laws.

[1]

God's sinners gather basking in his silence,

Free from judgement, bought with fake compliance,

With preachers that insult God's divine license

The flock is led astray: deceitful guidance.

[2]

By concealing facts of their shameful transgressions,

The church promotes sin through moral regression,

Absolving all their misdeeds and foul aggressions,

Neglecting the victims who live with oppression.

[3]

The sinner's paradise: complete secrecy, no shame,

Portraying their sincerity by playing the game,

Clinging to God's compassion, disregarding all blame,

Abusers without consequences, all in his name.

[4]

Our elders double down, supporting the abuse,

Claiming that shortcomings are a valid excuse

To protect the culprit, condemning the recluse,

Failing the innocent by ignoring the bruise.

[5]

Spreading God's grace with the church's hypocrisy,

Deflecting all the guilt through vile theocracy,

Preaching their rules made with blind democracy,

And for his glory they hide atrocities.

[6]

Despite the church's actions, forgiving their sins,

The masses spread rumours, torturing their kin,

Feigning virtue while the silent sinner's grin,

In this fable, only one character wins.

[7]

The children demoralized by their church's conduct,

Peace in their home they inadvertently abduct,

With experience they were able to deduct

Fallacies of forgiveness they like to construct.

[8]

The family moves forward disguising their disdain,

Indoctrinated in the culture of the insane,

An action-filled life story difficult to explain,

Many personal grievances they had to contain.

[9]

When sinners confess to the holy trinity,

They are often blessed with full impunity,

Laws which they bypass, discounting the gravity,

Fueling the ruse and the miscreants' liberty.

[10]

Birds of the same feather flocking together,

Hiding their grimace and stifling their laughter,

In God's refuge confessing at the altar,

Washing their sins away with dirty water.

15

FILIPINO CAREGIVER

THEMES

Privilege

Poverty

Parentification

Bonding

Hope

FORMAT

8 words per line

4 lines per stanza

10 stanzas total

RHYTHM

Syllables Per Stanza

The following entry speaks to the experience of the eldest Filipino child who has to assume responsibility for the care of his younger sibling. When parents immigrate for work, children can miss out on the experiences of a typical childhood. In the best circumstances, immediate family members are able to provide stability by absorbing some of the responsibilities unsatisfied by absent parents; in the worst case scenario, children can easily become isolated from the larger family unit. In these cases, it is common to see children taking the primary caregiver role to a younger sibling out of necessity. Today, abandonment remains a common fear for many children who are left behind. There are many children that experience anxiety while waiting for the next call or update from their parents. Although it is not the norm, there are Filipino immigrants that chose to leave behind their families and begin new lives.

[1]

The firstborn child is gifted with the "privilege"

Of raising his kin: a resource to leverage,

Working to elevate their lives in the village,

Striving for the future to preserve their lineage.

[2]

Most could not endure the great income disparity,

The product of a state of excessive poverty,

By ignoring our own needs in complete modesty,

Sowing the fields as a result of necessity.

[3]

Having limited options to avoid death by hunger,

The children are separated from their doting mother,

With a valid reason, his independence they plunder,

Parentification at five was all he could muster.

[4]

The brother and sister form an unbreakable bond,

Isolated from the rest but becoming more fond,

Hoping and believing their mother would not abscond,

Establishing their distance from the slough of despond.

[5]

For half a decade, he tolerated the pain,

Yearning for his mother, to caress her again,

Despite her absence, he moves forward and maintains

A positive outlook in order to stay sane.

[6]

The young big brother is tasked to oversee

His sister's survival, born when he was three;

A life of duty for the young detainee

Who leads with kindness in spite of absentees.

[7]

The son, "blessed" with the gift of experience,

Endured much torment while in exile, in silence

Doing what he could to give "parental" guidance,

He kept to himself, no complaints or defiance.

[8]

The siblings play together in the smouldering sun,

Enjoying the wild where their adventure had begun,

With an absent father who prioritizes his fun

And delegates his duties to his firstborn son.

[9]

Growing stronger with every moment that they share,

Conquering the hardship, despite the wear and tear,

By blessing each other with tender loving care,

The children adapt with little time to prepare.

[10]

For the silver lining, looking to the sky,

Imagining the day that they would soon fly,

Despite the obstacles he holds his head high,

And pays his dues without ever asking why.

AFTERWORD

I hope that you enjoyed the auditory and visual storytelling of my life and perspectives. As a writer and avid consumer of hip-hop culture, I wrote each composition with hip-hop and poetry fusion in mind. I attempt to find the optimal balance between oral storytelling, precise lyricism, and urban musicality in all the volumes of *The Modern Filipino*. The book cover illustration is an animalistic interpretation of the current flag of the Philippines, highlighting its colours (blue, red, and yellow) and distinctive forms (the sun). The Philippine Eagle is displayed in prominence to allude to the original tribes of the archipelago. The chapter illustrations are based on three themes: the Philippine Milkfish (the national fish of the Philippines), the Philippine Carabao (the national animal of the Philippines) and the Bahay Kubo (the traditional wood house of the Philippines). The national colours are especially emphasized in all of the graphic compositions.

AUTHOR

Bayani Catapang immigrated to Canada from the Philippines in 2004, along with his father and sister, to reunite with his mother, who had moved to the country for work in 1999. Today his nuclear family consists of five members: a father, a mother, the eldest child (brother, the protagonist), the middle child (sister), and the youngest child (sister). Catapang's father and mother come from similar backgrounds: humble families of working-class farmers and labourers. By acquiring higher education, they both overcame poverty (in its modern conceptualization) and eventually rose to the middle class of the Philippines. Both of Catapang's parents are successful professionals in their own regard: his father has a background in electrical engineering, mathematics, and post-secondary education, while his mother has a background in communications, nursing, post-secondary education, and social work.

The Catapang family lineage originates from the native inhabitants of the archipelago, with mixed lineages from separate ethnolinguistic tribal groups falling under the category of the "Ilocanos." Prior to the archipelago's colonization by the Spanish Empire, the various tribal communities of Luzon held similar ways of life: subsistence farming, hunting local wildlife, and practicing different variations of nature worship. The Catapangs speak Ilocano and Tagalog, the former being the Lingua Franca of the Luzon tribes while the latter is the most widely spoken indigenous language in Luzon (with an estimated 22 million native speakers). Today's version of the Tagalog language is a mixture of the original Tagalog tribe's language (approximately 55%), Spanish (approximately 30%), and English (approximately 15%).

BAYANICATAPANG.CA

INSTAGRAM @BAYANICATAPANG

Manufactured by Amazon.ca
Bolton, ON